Alexand
63 Fasci
For Kids

Phillip Walker

All rights reserved. No part of this publication may be reproduced in any form or by any means, including scanning, photocopying, or otherwise, without prior written permission of the copyright holder. Copyright Phillip Walker © 2024

This book is just one of a series of "Fascinating Facts For Kids" books. For more fascinating facts about people, history, animals, and much more, please visit:

www.fascinatingfactsforkids.com

Contents

Early Years.. 1
Bucephalas... 4
King Alexander.................................... 6
Invading Persia.................................... 8
The Battle of Issus............................. 11
The Siege of Tyre............................... 14
Egypt.. 16
Showdown with Darius..................... 18
King of Persia..................................... 20
India... 23
Discontent... 26
The Journey Home............................ 29
Death... 32
Illustration Attributions................... 35

Early Years

1. Prince Alexander was born in 356 BC in Macedonia, a small kingdom north of Ancient Greece. He was the son of Philip II, the King of Macedonia, and his wife, Queen Olympias.

2. Both Philip and Olympias claimed they were descended from heroes of Ancient Greek mythology – Olympias from the legendary Greek warrior Achilles, and Philip from Heracles, who was the son of Zeus, King of the Gods. From a young age, Alexander was aware of his connection with gods and heroes, and he grew up knowing that he was special and destined to achieve great things.

Zeus, King of the Gods

3. King Philip made sure that his son received the best education available. Alexander was taught to read, write, and perform arithmetic by the finest private tutors. In addition to his academic studies, Alexander learned to play the lyre, a small harp-like instrument popular in Ancient Greece. He was also trained in horse riding, hunting, and fighting with all kinds of weapons.

Playing the lyre

4. When Alexander was 13 years old, King Philip took his son's education to an even higher level by hiring the famous Greek philosopher, Aristotle, as Alexander's personal tutor. Under Aristotle's guidance, Alexander studied philosophy, science, and politics, gaining a deep understanding of these subjects that would serve him well in the future.

Bucephalas

5. By the age of 12, Alexander had become an expert horseman and was keen to have a horse of his own. One day, a horse dealer offered to sell King Philip a wild horse, claiming it was the finest in the world. The horse, named Bucephalas, was completely black except for a distinctive white mark on his forehead.

6. However, Bucephalas was too highly strung and impossible to ride, and so King Philip refused to buy the horse. Alexander, however, was convinced that he could tame Bucephalas, and he persuaded his father to let him try.

7. Alexander had noticed that Bucephalas was frightened by his own shadow. To calm the horse, Alexander took hold of the reins and calmly walked Bucephalas toward the sun, so that the horse's shadow was behind him and out of sight.

Alexander and Bucephalas

8. After a short while, Alexander successfully mounted Bucephalas and galloped off. King Philip was very impressed by his son's horsemanship and agreed to buy Bucephalas for Alexander. From then on, Bucephalas would remain Alexander's loyal companion, accompanying him on his military campaigns and adventures for the next 20 years.

King Alexander

9. When he was just 16 years old, Alexander took charge of Macedonia while his father was away on a military campaign. Shortly after King Philip's departure, Macedonia was invaded by an army from the neighboring kingdom of Thrace.

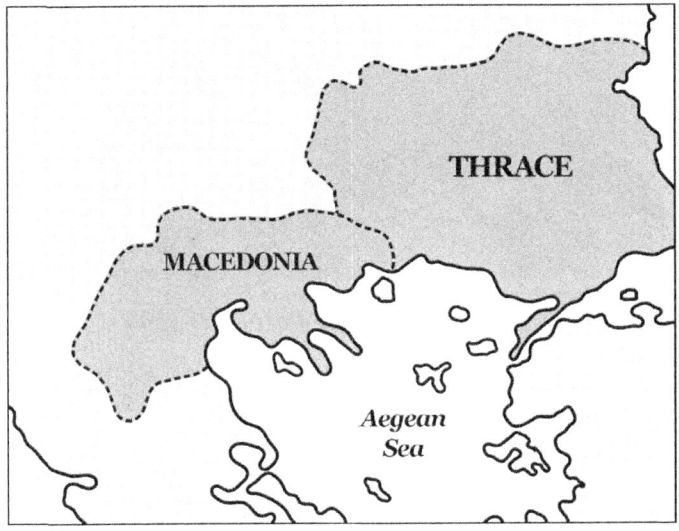

10. Alexander quickly assembled an army and led his troops against the invaders. Despite his youth, Alexander was a natural leader and tactically brilliant, and the enemy was beaten easily. This victory marked the first of many successful military campaigns Alexander would lead throughout his life.

11. From that point on, Alexander and his father often led the Macedonian army together. When war broke out between Macedonia and the

Greek city-state of Athens in 339 BC, Philip and Alexander fought alongside each other, and after a year of fierce fighting, they led Macedonia to victory. King Philip now became the ruler of the whole of Greece and was at the height of his powers.

12. With Greece under his control, Philip set his sights on a new target – the Persian Empire. He planned to invade Persia in revenge for its invasion of Greece 150 years earlier. However, this ambitious plan was cut short when Philip was assassinated by one of his bodyguards.

13. Philip's death meant that Alexander, at the age of just 20, was now King of Macedonia and the ruler of Greece. But despite his young age, Alexander was well-prepared for the role, having proven himself as an excellent military leader, earning the respect and loyalty of his soldiers.

Invading Persia

14. As the newly-crowned king, Alexander decided to carry out his father's ambition of waging war against the Persian Empire. The empire was huge, stretching from the Mediterranean Sea in the west to present-day Pakistan in the east, and a successful conquest would establish Alexander as the most powerful ruler in the world.

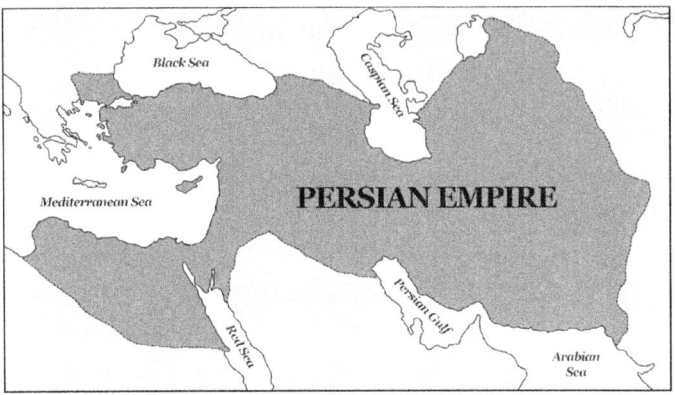

15. Over the course of a year, Alexander assembled a mighty army, made up of men from both Macedonia and Greece. In the spring of 334 BC, thousands of soldiers boarded a fleet of ships and set sail for present-day Turkey, a region that was then part of the Persian Empire.

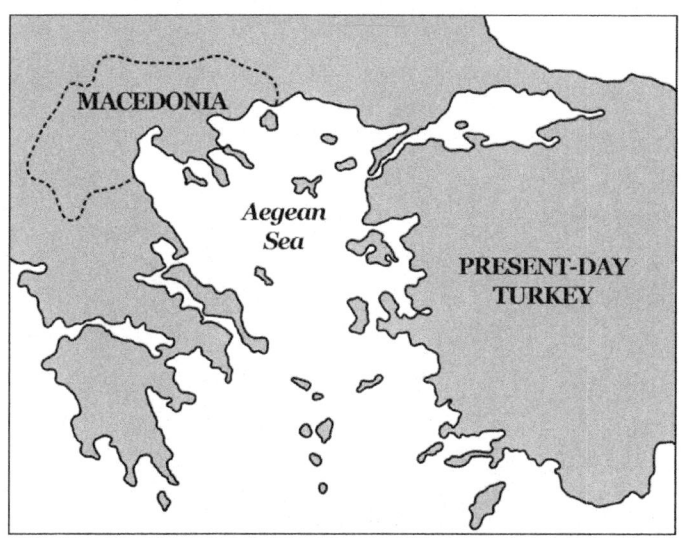

16. Upon reaching land, Alexander and his army marched south until they encountered the Persian army on the opposite bank of the Granicus River. Alexander's troops found a shallow section of the river, crossed to the other side, and launched a fierce charge against the Persians. Despite being outnumbered, the ferocity and skill of Alexander's soldiers quickly overwhelmed the enemy.

Fighting at the Battle of Granicus

17. Following the decisive victory at the Battle of the Granicus, Alexander and his army continued their march south. They encountered resistance along the way, although many of the cities they arrived at welcomed Alexander as a liberator, freeing them from 200 years of Persian rule.

The Battle of Issus

18. Following the victory at the Granicus River, Alexander and his army spent the following few months taking control of Asia Minor (present-day Turkey). In late 333 BC, as they advanced deeper into Persian territory, they encountered a massive Persian army near the town of Issus. It was led by Darius III, the King of Persia himself.

Darius III

19. Despite being outnumbered by the Persians, Alexander's troops were far better trained and more disciplined. And Alexander's tactical brilliance and leadership skills were far superior to those of Darius, giving the Macedonians a critical advantage on the battlefield.

20. As the battle commenced, Alexander's army demonstrated its superior tactics and fighting abilities. Armed with long spears and protected by shields, the Macedonians crowded together in tightly packed formations before attacking and quickly overwhelming the enemy.

Macedonian soldiers in formation

21. Darius soon realized that he was facing defeat, and made the decision to flee the battlefield. Without their leader, he Persian army soon lost heart and began to crumble. Many soldiers fled, while others were captured or killed. In the end, Alexander was victorious, having inflicted a crushing defeat on a numerically superior enemy.

22. In his haste to escape, Darius had left behind his family, including his mother, wife, and children, as well as an enormous amount of treasure. The capture of the royal family and the Persian riches was a powerful symbol of Alexander's triumph and further demoralized the Persian forces.

Alexander with the family of Darius

The Siege of Tyre

23. Following the victory at the Battle of Issus, Alexander set his sights on taking on the Persian navy that dominated the Mediterranean Sea. As he did not have enough ships to fight the Persians in a naval battle, Alexander decided to capture the ports that supplied the Persian fleet with essential supplies of food and water.

24. The first two ports Alexander arrived at, Byblos and Sidon, surrendered without a fight. However, when the Macedonian army reached the city of Tyre, they were met with fierce resistance. The people of Tyre, confident in the strength of their defences and the support of the Persian navy, refused to surrender.

25. Tyre was located on an island just off the coast, making it difficult for Alexander's army to reach. To overcome this problem, the

Macedonians began the construction of a half-mile-long (1 km) causeway from the mainland to the island, using stones and timber from the surrounding area.

26. As the causeway neared completion, attacks were launched from Tyre on the Macedonians to stop them from reaching the island. However, Alexander's men fought back, firing stones and red-hot pieces of metal from giant catapults so that the building work could continue. When the causeway was eventually finished, the Macedonians used battering rams to smash down the city walls before fighting their way into the city.

27. After a fierce and bloody struggle, Alexander emerged victorious, but at a heavy cost, with many of his men being killed in the battle. Enraged by Tyre's resistance and the casualties his army had suffered, Alexander ordered the execution of a large number of the city's inhabitants. This brutal act served as a warning to other cities that might consider defying his authority.

Egypt

28. After the successful Siege of Tyre, Alexander turned his attention toward Egypt, the wealthiest region of the Persian Empire. For centuries, the country had been ruled by Egyptian kings, known as pharaohs, until the Persians invaded and took control in 525 BC.

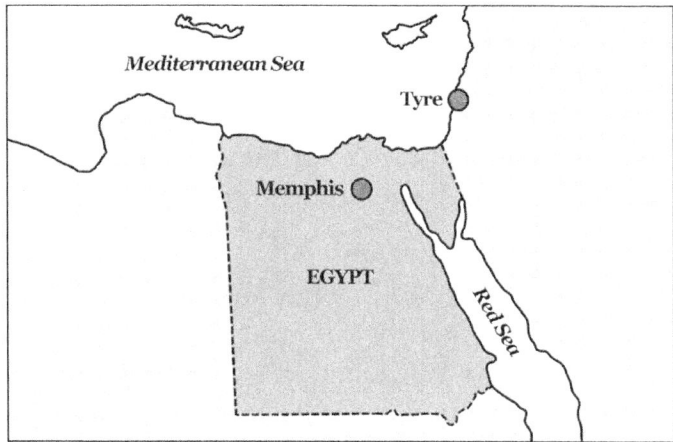

29. The Egyptians deeply resented Persian rule and had long yearned for independence. When Alexander arrived at the Egyptian capital, Memphis, he was greeted as a liberator rather than a conqueror. The Egyptians were so overjoyed to be freed from Persian domination that they made Alexander their new pharaoh.

30. As the new ruler of Egypt, Alexander decided to build a new capital city on the Mediterranean coast which would be called Alexandria. It was the first of many cities throughout the Persian Empire that Alexander would name after himself.

31. The construction of Alexandria began in 331 BC, with Alexander overseeing the layout of the streets, the placement of key buildings, and the development of a harbor. The city was designed to be a center of trade, learning, and culture, and it attracted scholars, artists, and merchants from across Europe, Asia, and Africa. Alexandria's importance continued long after Alexander's death, and it remained a significant center of the ancient world for centuries. It still stands today, a thriving city on Egypt's Mediterranean coastline more than 2,000 years later.

Alexandria today

Showdown with Darius

32. After a six-month stay in Egypt, Alexander set out to confront King Darius once more. The Persian king had spent the intervening time strengthening his army and was now waiting for Alexander on a vast, dusty plain near the village of Gaugamela in present-day Iraq.

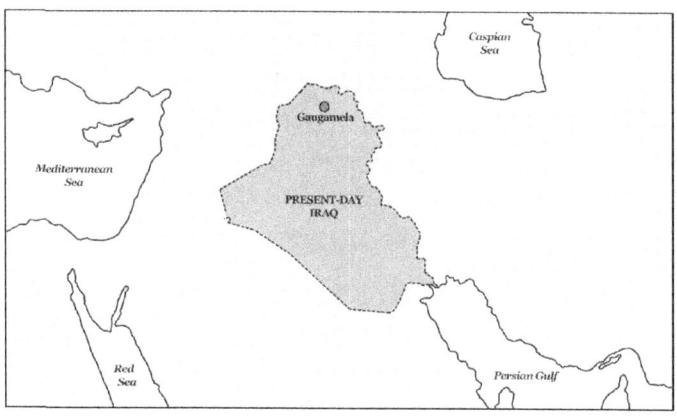

33. When the two armies met, it was clear that Darius's army was much bigger than Alexander's. However, Alexander's soldiers were battle-hardened and had complete faith in their commander's ability to lead them to victory.

34. The Battle of Gaugamela began with a fierce clash of cavalry and infantry. The Persians fought bravely, but Alexander gradually gained the upper hand. He personally led a daring charge against Darius's position, causing the Persian king to panic and flee the battlefield, just as he had done at Issus.

35. Seeing the Persian king's retreat, Alexander galloped after him on Bucephalas. However, Darius had a considerable head start, and despite their best efforts, Alexander and Bucephalas could not catch him. Darius managed to escape, leaving his army to face defeat at the hands of the Macedonians.

36. The Battle of Gaugamela marked a decisive victory for Alexander, and it established his reputation as one of the greatest military commanders the world had seen. Although Darius had escaped, his army lay in ruins, and Alexander was free to march on the great cities at the heart of the empire and declare himself King of Persia.

King of Persia

37. After his decisive victory at Gaugamela, only the eastern provinces of the Persian Empire remained to be conquered. He marched his army eastward to the great cities of Babylon, Susa, and Persepolis, which all surrendered and welcomed the Macedonians without resistance.

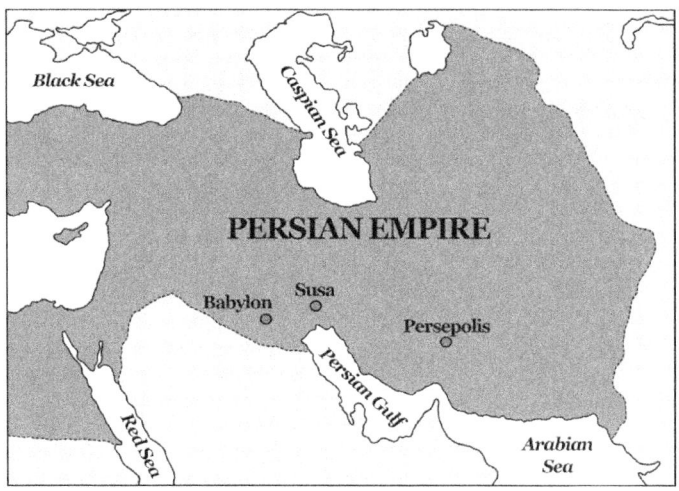

38. In order to be accepted as the King of Persia, Alexander began to adopt Persian customs and habits. He started wearing Persian clothing and surrounded himself with Persian courtiers and advisors. This change in behavior saw Alexander become increasingly pompous and arrogant. He sat on a golden throne and expected both Persians and Macedonians to bow before him.

39. The Macedonians resented the changes in their leader's behavior, particularly his expectation that they, too, should adopt Persian ways. Alexander, however, was unaware of their growing discontent until an incident at a party he held for some of his officers.

40. During the party, one of Alexander's officers, Cleitus, became drunk and began to criticize Alexander's new behavior. Cleitus even went so far as to say that Alexander's father, Philip, had been a better man than Alexander could ever be. Enraged by these comments, Alexander, who was also drunk, seized a spear and killed Cleitus on the spot.

Cleitus criticizing Alexander

41. The murder of Cleitus deeply shocked Alexander's soldiers. They had witnessed not just a change in their leader's personality, but had also seen him commit a terrible act in a drunken fit of anger. From then on, the relationship between Alexander and his men would never be the same.

India

42. After conquering the Persian Empire, many of Alexander's followers hoped that he would finally take a rest after a decade of continuous warfare. However, Alexander had different plans. In 326 BC, he led his army eastward, intent on conquering India.

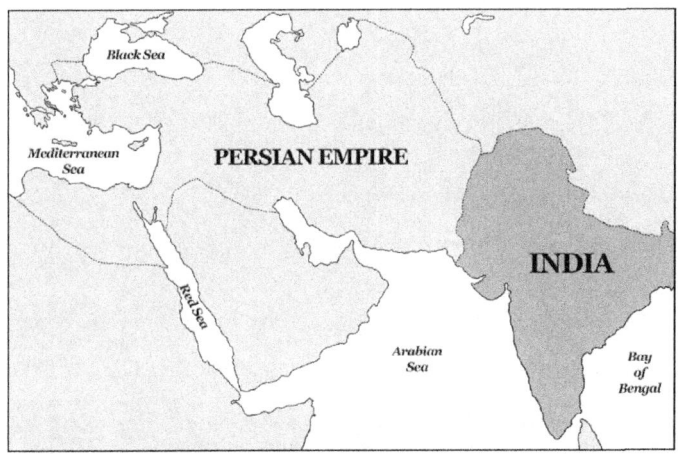

43. The people of India had no desire to be ruled by a foreign king, and they prepared to resist Alexander's invasion. An Indian king named Poros gathered an army of 50,000 men and waited for the Macedonians at the banks of the River Hydaspes (now the River Jhelum) near the border of India and the Persian Empire.

44. Despite the massive size of the Indian army, Alexander was confident of victory. He led his army across the river and attacked Poros's forces. The Indian soldiers fought bravely, but

Alexander's tactics and the discipline of his troops once again proved superior. The defeat of Poros and his enormous army was perhaps Alexander's greatest military achievement.

Poros surrenders to Alexander

45. However, the joy of victory was short-lived. Soon after the battle, Alexander's beloved horse, Bucephalas, died. The stallion had been Alexander's faithful companion for nearly 20 years, carrying him through many battles and campaigns. Alexander was heartbroken by the loss of his trusted steed.

46. To honor Bucephalas, Alexander held a grand funeral ceremony fit for a hero. He then ordered the construction of a new city on the site where the horse was buried. The city was named Bucephala, a lasting tribute to the animal that had been so important to Alexander.

47. Following Bucephalas's funeral, Alexander continued eastward through India. But his army, exhausted from years of campaigning and far from home, grew reluctant to press further into unknown lands. Alexander, however, remained determined to carry on and reach the very edge of the known world, becoming the greatest conqueror of all time.

Discontent

48. Alexander's timing for the invasion of India couldn't have been worse. It was the start of the summer monsoon season, a time when heavy rains fall continuously for three months. Day after day, the army had to march through thick mud, and were constantly soaked to the skin by the relentless downpour. Their clothes rotted away, and their weapons rusted. Many men died after being bitten by poisonous snakes that were looking for dry land.

49. The region Alexander chose to march through was known as the Punjab, a name meaning "land of the five rivers." The heavy rains had swollen these rivers, turning them into fast-flowing, treacherous waterways. As the army crossed the first four rivers, many soldiers were swept away by the strong currents or attacked by crocodiles.

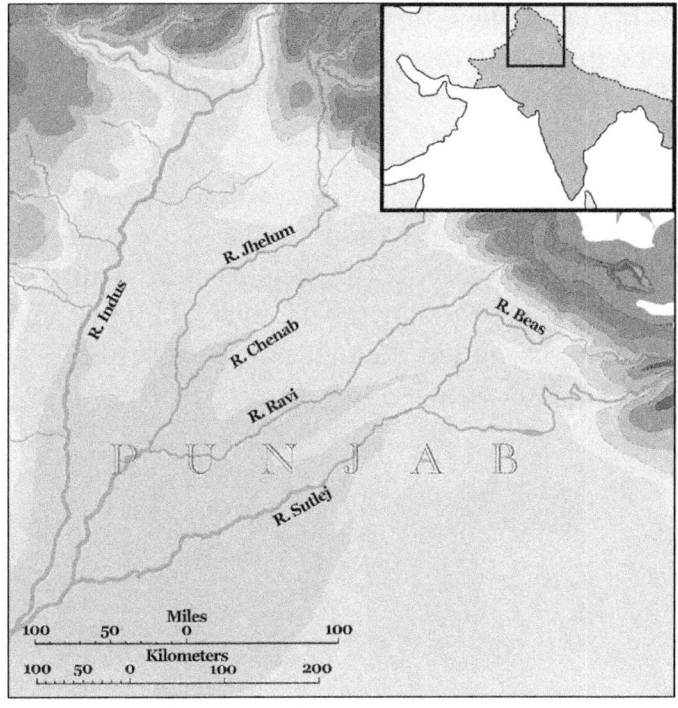

"Land of the Five Rivers"

50. When they reached the fifth river, the River Beas, Alexander's exhausted troops had reached breaking point. They refused to cross, demanding instead to return home to Macedonia. The men had endured years of the constant fighting and now they faced the hardships of the monsoon season. What they wanted now was the comfort and familiarity of their homeland.

51. Alexander was furious with his soldiers' refusal to continue the campaign and retreated to his tent, where he sulked for three days, refusing to talk to anyone. The great conqueror, who had never before been defied by his own men, was faced with a mutiny.

52. Eventually, Alexander was forced to accept the reality of the situation. He could not continue his campaign without the support of his army, and he realized that carrying on would only lead to more discontent. Reluctantly, he agreed to lead his men back home.

The Journey Home

53. Alexander decided to take a different route back, so that he could explore more of the region. He led his army south toward the Indian Ocean, encountering some of the most warlike tribes in India along the way.

54. During one particularly fierce battle, Alexander was struck in the chest by an arrow, causing him to lose a large amount of blood. He came close to death, and his men feared they would never make it home without their leader's guidance. However, Alexander slowly recovered and was eventually able to continue the journey, much to the relief of his soldiers.

55. When he reached the coast, Alexander divided his army into three groups. One group would travel by ship, exploring the coastal waters. Alexander himself would lead a second group across the vast and barren Gedrosian Desert. The third group, made up of older soldiers, would take a safer and easier route further north. The plan was for all three groups to meet at the eastern end of the Persian Gulf, before heading north together for the city of Susa.

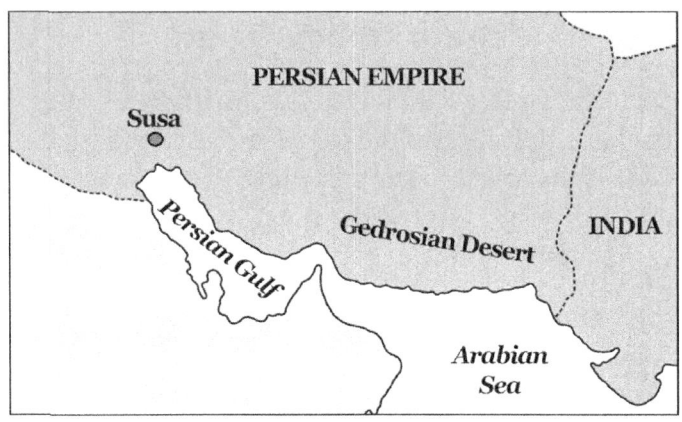

56. The reasons behind Alexander's decision to march through the desert are uncertain. He may have been punishing his men for their earlier mutiny in India, or maybe he simply wanted to be the first person to successfully cross the Gedrosian Desert. Whatever the reason, the journey proved to be highly challenging. It took two grueling months, and thousands of Alexander's men died from thirst and hunger in the scorching desert heat.

57. Eventually, Alexander's army reached Susa, where a mass wedding ceremony was held. Alexander himself married two members of the Persian royal family. Additionally, he arranged for 90 of his officers to marry the daughters of Persian noblemen. Alexander hoped these marriages would help bring the Persians and Macedonians closer together. However, his men were unhappy about being forced to marry

Persian women when they longed to return home to their families in Macedonia.

Death

58. Alexander left Susa in the spring of 324 BC and spent the rest of the year in the mountain city of Ecbatana, where the weather was cooler. In the spring of 323 BC, he moved on to Babylon, where he began planning further conquests. Despite already ruling the largest empire the world had ever seen, Alexander was not satisfied and wanted even more.

59. Alexander decided to invade Arabia and all of North Africa west of Egypt, before moving on to conquer Spain and Italy. When the preparations for the Arabian invasion were complete, Alexander ordered a grand celebration to mark the occasion.

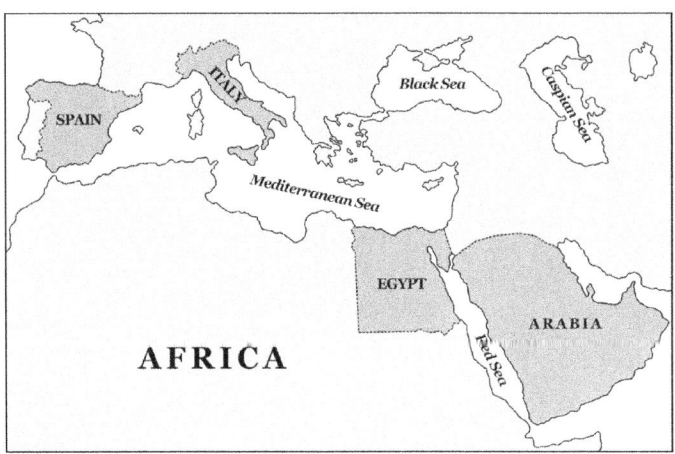

60. The following morning, Alexander awoke with a high fever. His condition quickly deteriorated, and it soon became apparent that

Alexander was on his deathbed. As he lay dying, his closest friends gathered around him and asked, "To whom do you leave your empire?" With his last remaining strength, Alexander replied, "To the strongest." Shortly after uttering these final words, Alexander the Great died at the age of just 32.

61. Following Alexander's death, the Macedonians spent an entire year planning his funeral and building a magnificent carriage to transport his body back to Macedonia. When the funeral procession finally set off, the carriage was pulled by a team of 64 mules and escorted by hundreds of Alexander's soldiers. Enormous crowds gathered along the route to catch a final glimpse of their king.

Alexander's funeral procession

62. However, Alexander's body never reached its intended destination. Ptolemy, one of

Alexander's generals who had become the ruler of Egypt, seized the carriage and took it to Memphis. Alexander's body remained there for 40 years before it was moved once more, this time to Alexandria. There, it was housed in a grand mausoleum, which soon became a place of pilgrimage, attracting visitors from across the known world.

63. Tragically, in 365 AD, Alexandria was struck by a devastating tidal wave caused by a massive undersea earthquake near the island of Crete, some 400 miles (650 km) across the Mediterranean Sea. In the aftermath of this disaster, Alexander's tomb vanished from the face of the earth. Its exact location was lost to history, and despite numerous attempts to rediscover it over the centuries, the final resting place of Alexander the Great remains unknown to this day.

Illustration Attributions

Cover
Image by Gordon Johnson from Pixabay

Title page
Ny Carlsberg Glyptotek, Public domain, via Wikimedia Commons
{{PD-US}}
https://creativecommons.org/licenses/by/4.0/deed.en
https://creativecommons.org/licenses/by/4.0/legalcode.en

Zeus, King of the Gods
Image by Raphael from Pixabay

Playing the lyre
Staatliche Antikensammlungen, Public domain, via Wikimedia Commons

Alexander and Bucephalas
Domenico Maria Canuti, Public domain, via Wikimedia Commons
{{PD-US}}

Fighting at the Battle of Granicus
Charles Le Brun, Public domain, via Wikimedia Commons
{{PD-US}}

Darius III
Carole Raddato from FRANKFURT, Germany, CC BY-SA 2.0
<https://creativecommons.org/licenses/by-sa/2.0>, via Wikimedia Commons
https://creativecommons.org/licenses/by-sa/2.0/deed.en
https://creativecommons.org/licenses/by-sa/2.0/legalcode.en

Macedonian soldiers in formation
Edmund OllierPublication date 1882, Public domain, via Wikimedia Commons
{{PD-US}}

Alexander with the family of Darius
Justus Sustermans, Public domain, via Wikimedia Commons
{{PD-US}}

Alexandria today
Abdelrhman 1990, CC BY-SA 4.0
<https://creativecommons.org/licenses/
by-sa/4.0>, via Wikimedia Commons
https://creativecommons.org/licenses/
by-sa/4.0/deed.en
https://creativecommons.org/licenses/
by-sa/4.0/legalcode.en

Cleitus criticizing Alexander
Weston, W H; Plutarch; Rainey, W, Public domain, via Wikimedia Commons
{{PD-US}}

Poros surrenders to Alexander
Alonzo Chappel, Public domain, via Wikimedia Commons
{{PD-US}}

"Land of the Five Rivers"
Apuldram, CC BY-SA 3.0
<https://creativecommons.org/licenses/
by-sa/3.0>, via Wikimedia Commons
https://creativecommons.org/licenses/
by-sa/3.0/deed.en
https://creativecommons.org/licenses/
by-sa/3.0/legalcode.en
(changes made)

Printed in Great Britain
by Amazon

45120297R00030